Michael Knox

THE NORTH END POEMS

ECW PRESS

MISFIT

Published by ECW Press, 2120 Queen Street East, Suite 200,
Toronto, Ontario, Canada M4E 1E2
416.694.3348 / info@ecwpress.com

LIBRARY AND ARCHIVES CANADA CATALOGUING IN PUBLICATION

Knox, Michael, 1978–
The North End poems / Michael Knox.

"a misFit book."
ISBN 978-1-55022-817-5

1. Title.

PS8621.N69N67 2008   C811'.6   C2007-907104-X

Editor for the press: Michael Holmes / a misFit book
Type: Rachel Brooks
Cover Design: David Gee
Author photo: Shanaeh Reid
Printing: Coach House Printing

This book is set in Bembo, TradeGothic and CgDeVinne

The publication of *The North End Poems* has been generously supported by the Canada
Council for the Arts, which last year invested $20.1 million in writing and publishing
throughout Canada, by the Ontario Arts Council, by the Government of Ontario
through Ontario Book Publishing Tax Credit, by the OMDC Book Fund, an initiative of
the Ontario Media Development Corporation, and by the Government of Canada
through the Book Publishing Industry Development Program (BPIDP).

 Canada Council   Conseil des Arts
for the Arts   du Canada
Canadä    ONTARIO ARTS COUNCIL
CONSEIL DES ARTS DE L'ONTARIO

PRINTED AND BOUND IN CANADA

ECW PRESS
ecwpress.com

MISFIT

For Ali and for Andrea, who stay in this scrap.

THE NORTH END POEMS

CHARACTERS

The Macfarlanes

Nick
Jimmy — Nick's Father
Ricky — Nick's Uncle
Johnny — Nick's Uncle
Chad — Nick's younger brother

The Boys

K — Nick's best friend
Scotty — Nick's friend
Ronnie — Nick's friend

The Girls

Carla — Nick's girlfriend
Kasia — Carla's housemate

The Rest

Jen — Ronnie's girlfriend
Cora — daughter of Ronnie and Jen
Helen — Johnny's ex-wife
Lincoln — Nick's sparring partner
Ronan — Ronnie's father
Steven — Carla's teenage brother

THE HARBOUR AT EVENING

Water gnaws the shore
industrial black blurring
wobbling smokestacks.
The bulk of the steel mills
and the blotting faces of men
who stand and smoke unnoticing.

Clang of industry
faint but ubiquitous
dusk has settled shadows
filling their songless faces.
Life is withstanding.

Pinched cigarettes
three beers that interfere with sleep
the dubious constancy
of wives and children

and awful fraternity
always that.

Mangy seagulls wheel in pursuit
flash of a nemesis
matching every careening
winking out of being
slips over the dock
flutters stiffly to the lip
of one of the rusted trashcans
strung along the quay.

Severe eye like a hard drop of blood
a cry like a burst of hell.
The men smoke and watch
ships tiny in their world

of open ocean, huge in this one.
Hong Kong Vancouver Cape Town
a thousand lives like theirs.

NORTH END SONNET

The city dives from itself floating half aloft.
Steel-fires beneath illuminate gutted porches that watch and think.
Barred doors and broken windows bleed the night air draft.
Waist-high weeds poke through chain-link.

Drinks and laughter on the dirt front lawn.
Knees snap pool cues in cloudy halls, splintered keen.
Glaring white kids stand in packs with open noses, then come on.
Bass buzz lopes from tinted Cutlass Supremes.

Discarded blankets weather against brick factories, skeletons of bikes.
Women with sunken cheeks and slow, squalid wrath.
Eighteen-wheelers shiver roadside weeds and houses alike.
Railway lots seem abandoned but sprout trash.

Fresh tattoos leak from ship cable arms, blood inside wrecked.
Scabbing hands quiver first of the month cheques.

ENTER NICK

Nick squints his way
down Burlington Street.

Transports heavy sprint past
rolls of steel
beds of stone
machines uncannily perched.
Things that wear men's hands.

Steel toes stump
by industrial yards.
The smell of exhaust
grey belch of steel fire.

Nick stretches a stiff bicep
drags a key through fresh chain-link
spits high over its barbed crown
into the smashed skids.

He crosses Wellington without looking
North End swagger and long stare
down the empty street
before he climbs his front stairs.

SUMMER WORDS

Meet us menacing
in the wide-skied evening
with the slap of laughter
sunset angling our squinting
bottles amber cores
in callused princely grips.

Problems and solutions
have their genesis here.

We still cut each other's hair in K's yard
wrench on bucket cars
instead of second-hand bikes
scrap with the same kids
over new nonsense
colonize the same steps
talk shit day and night.

The sound of ships inching in the harbour
dusk off the railway tracks
between houses
from dockyards
that point to Toronto and Montreal.

The architecture of our lives
in porch dialogue and sermons
in the stories we spin and believe
in the lens our talk fits firmly over our lives.

TEN YEARS
Jimmy

Ten years

dreams are ghosts
that visit with hangovers:

manic ciphers
nothing or everything
to do with her.

She's changed everything
even sleep.

He is himself
or not himself
or no one

and she is herself
or not herself
or everyone

and the desperation
of horrifying comedies

sickening offspring
of his waking.

Absence is her epitaph

a whisper
across the landscape of sleep.

WE DON'T TIP

K's eyelids are a sprawl, in a sleeveless shirt
he leans across the bar
and hollers to the barman for an Export.
Wide back to him, opportunity there
brown bottle finds someone else's tip
slides it home to K, a slow tumble
from the edge to his grip.
Smooth switch to his pocket, no metallic mumble.

He pays the barman and walks off.
"How about a tip, buddy!" met with a laugh.

Not even turning, K throws back his head,
crowing, "Here's a tip, pal: don't smoke in bed."

WALKING THE TRACKS HOME

The night tangible,
the moon large and pale
shines the rails.
I toss my last bottle back.
The shatter, a quick crack
on the rods put here by Scottish hands
connecting and creating this vast land.

Dormant houses and dark factories below;
a screen of silence hangs
over siding and brick, now slowed
the harbour whispers where today it sang.
Cheery rooms glow yellow
promise sleep still
stretching over shadowed sills.

No moon suddenly, a dream
vanishing
in a vault of steam
that connects to steel mills
cords of smoke chugging up, away
from stacks like candles that puff
over a toy landscape.

CHURCH

Spring to fall Jimmy makes the numb trek
from the pub
sometimes pauses on the steps
of the Presbyterian church
to smoke in the first or second hour of Sunday.

His great grandfather was a professor in Glasgow,
a theologian; everything he knows
has the old man hunched
in a blanket by the fire reading the Bible.

A vulture's face,
judgmental, hungering,
intense and pious Scrooge.
The fire is huge and alive,
the family quiet about his reading,
the night outside filled with God's eyes.

Jimmy's lived with this image since he was a boy
and has never tried to dismantle it,
understand it further than he does.
Distaste for religion learned from a father
who hated his guilt and its reinforcements.

Jimmy feels the nightfilled church:
its watch of steady unwelcome.
And walks the rest of the way home
hands deep in his pockets.

COFFEE ALONE
Jimmy

Sunday morning, the kitchen
a tender grey,
flutter of rain
in the trees out back
gently nowhere.
No disturbance
in the sleeping world.

This is where loss is most acute.

If she were here now
we'd have two mugs at the table;
I'd read and not watch the window.

I stand there now
try to marvel like she did
hugging herself in her housecoat
the chatter from the leaves
quiet company of mist.

I can't even bring myself to open the paper
as if I'd be ignoring
the only real traces of her.

JIMMY AT WORK

In the yard backhoes
scoop slithering stone.

Coffee cups mound inside rusted bins, Styrofoam
crowned briefly with gulls, maniac-eyed.
Cigarette butts seed a brown lawn.

The lunchroom is untidy as a nursery
fetid with sweat, dust-caked fingertips, traces in their lunches
and on nicotine yellowed lips.

Wrinkles, silvering mustaches and paunches
are all they are some days. Dignity is a vice, bullshit
that depends on diet and rest. Ungrammatical and obscene

they know they are anecdotes to the university students
new every other summer, who feign,
quick to proclaim their enthusiasm for unions,

who ride bikes home to young skin,
to small panties and blond ponytails on pillows.
At least that's what's assumed in silence.

The men smoke stonily at punch-in, like teenagers they crow
with coffee at first break, coughing by day's end
and the evening's pints of anesthetic, shit brew

a life of endurance
for ideals they were told were true.
Mistakes fathers were too ashamed not to make

propping huge machines with their elbows, fair weather brethren
joke most readily about what makes them most afraid:
cancer, retirement, gay sons, women.

BEFORE THE GYM

losing work gear
that will harden
to a knot of bark
then stretching
on a beaten mattress
the first ease
Nick finds today

he imagines
flesh into sand
into oblivion
feet then shins knees

until he is empty
for an hour's sleep

NEVER FORGET
Ronnie

Friday night's pay finds us
beers and shots between jokes at the rippers
pretending the orbits of hips don't depress us.
The hypocrisy: affirming we don't care
but spending volumes while we're at it.

K in his glory, dusting his blond head
a North End aristocrat twitching an occasional bicep.
I wonder if Jen has put Cora to bed.
Jen's ice, and like these women strutting;
it's sex I can't touch
the things I've lost before me
and guilt that I shouldn't be here.

Slipping down the rye someone's bought
I look up. I know the stripper.
Marianne something, lived up the street.
The familiarity repels me.
I wonder what happened to the baby
she dropped out pregnant with in grade 9;
if that bully who gave it to her stuck around.

The place closes and we're drunker than I thought in the parking lot.
A bouncer walks Marianne out and Nick sees her.
He breaks away from us and approaches her disarmingly
Marianne! It's Nick Macfarlane. Holy shit.

They dated when we were ten;
he still talks like she was the best girl he ever met.
I never had the heart to tell him what I knew
about her stepfather, why she probably meant
her boyfriend to get her pregnant.
People are fucked.

A Buick pulls in

I swear to god it's the same bucket her boyfriend used to drive
when he wasn't kicking kids' asses or making them piss their pants.
It pulls to the back of the lot
and I can see Marianne heading towards it.
Nick walks with her, still chatting.
The bouncer, figuring she's fine, heads back to the bar.

K's eyes get keen all at once —
he's drunker than the rest of us —
when he sees the Buick and the shadow step out.
Snarls, *Fuck is that?* like he already knows.

Todd Brown, somebody says.

Guy broke my Walkman and my nose in grade six,
laughed that my mom was dead. Fuck'n *laughed*.
Alchemy in the silence that follows, leadening his words.

You can feel hate, a vapour, rising from the pavement.
I want to say something but he's already on his way.
We follow at a couple of paces.

Nick is talking quietly to Marianne by the car.
K shoulders past, going right for Todd.
Hey, Todd. Remember me? Thumping shove against the car.
Said you'd piss on my mom's grave? Another shove.
Hands come up in bewildered apology, Todd stammering.

Hey, Todd, Scotty taunts, cracking knuckles, closing in,
you still tough?

We're all around him now. Steam of fury all over my skin.
Nick and Marianne both trying to get in the way
K head-butts Todd, dives on him when he drops.

Scotty's in a frenzy, rabid encouragement
holding Nick off with his back, pretending it's unintentional.
K punches and punches and there's whimpering.
K growls shit the whole time he unloads. You had it fuck'n come'n!
Rape my mom's corpse? Remember? Who's the fuck'n corpse now?
Marianne is bawling and pleading but it's like K can't hear anything.

Nick's voice: K, he's got a little daughter.

As though sobering, K looks at Nick,
like it's just the two of them.
Weak, abject, a little boy again.
He told me once he wanted to dig up my mom, dig her up and . . .

If you didn't have that kid,
K says, tears coming, I'd cut your fuck'n eyes out.
Never fucking forget.

DEEP
K

His body didn't have the weight I expected
he stooped slightly into my fist

the hardest thing
is not backing off
but there was hate
and hate is gluttonous

you hit him like it's never
enough
so hard something in him shatters
and you'd almost apologize

but you've learned that
there is life in this
much as anything else

a rapture in wrath
in this reptilian life

BOXING

Summer nights Nick cycles
through sunset streets
to the basement gym
on the same rusty mountain bike
he got second-hand
in the seventh grade.

Nostalgic North End fathers
pulse butch smugness
he was born into: eager
son with schoolyard black eyes.

For reluctant single mothers
the trainers become ringmasters
with carnival promises,
"Safest sport in the world!"
The mothers smile
while men just like those they left
belly laugh from the wings.

Nick skips then shadow boxes.
His trainer watches, offers the occasional
"Hitch at the waist. Hitch the hips."
Nick winks at Lincoln,
descending the stairs, always late.

Cycloning the bag to stay warm
Nick throws aggression out,
saving the rational technician.

Lincoln wears ease
spends half an hour socializing.
A flirt liked by everyone.
Nick overhears the same jokes:

"My head skips like my busted CD player,"
"You couldn't hit me with a flashlight beam."
He dances in headphones to warm up
then screams over them
"Yo, Macfarlane! Ring the bell,
school's in session!"

Nick picks headgear from the rack
pulls the moist lump of it around his head,
pumps two sixteen-ounce gloves together
and slips through the ropes.

Lincoln hasn't even got his wrists wrapped,
he sits on a bench and doesn't look once
at Nick's footwork while he binds them.

The only time Lincoln is expressionless
is sparring. The stark bell clenches his focus,
punctuates the present,
and he flies to meet Nick in the centre.

LINCOLN

Get in here, Macfarlane,
why you gotta keep my shit wait'n?
You know I'm a racehorse held back.
Baby, I live to get into it.

I want your best four rounds, bitch.
I want to taste your whole arsenal.
Baby, you'll feel me in your jaw
in the morning. And know I love you.

Fear ain't something I understand.
My hands are clean
and they burn for you, Macfarlane.
Getting hurt hurts but that's all.

People talk about this shit
like it's all fear and need.
Nah, baby, I'm a sorcerer;
you, my young apprentice.

Feel 'em thwacks, them shudders
I'm pumping into your headgear?
I'm just teasing your shit, letcha know
I'm the one doing the fucking winning.

I feel that desperation, see it in those eyes.
That wind I'm sapping out your lungs,
that strength out them stringy shoulders,
where's your heart now? How about now?

I don't even take you seriously, Macfarlane
and I can see your soul in your pupils. Fear me.
That's what I want. Feel that? Feel that?
Ooo, baby, I love it when you hurt me back.

Pray for that bell, baby. Pray.
Ain't for nothin' I'm Ontario champion.
I could hammer you in one numb crush,
deliver you like a preacher from time's grip.

K

With sand-filled dumbbells
K creates an imperial self.

Paces miles in this basement
breathing deep
between sets, nudging
spare plates on the floor
squeezing gently swelling
arms and chest,
centipedes scuttle
across the ceiling
throat of cool water
pick-tearing calluses.

His world framed
with dreaming
— *feeling* like certainty —
himself firefighting some day.
Consciousness laced with
starting to run,
training carrying awkward objects,
looking into courses.

It's here he believes he is not his father,
a man who let his mistakes happen to him.

HAIRCUT

K mows clippers over Nick's bowed head
with a brother's rough love

plants a callused hand on Nick's neck
steadying him and talks the whole time
like a real barber.

They leave the hair where it falls
let it mix with the soil.

Nick runs the tracks home shirtless
the breeze blowing stubble
sparks from his shoulders and arms
in the wash of the setting sun.

THE TANK

K's mud-coloured '82 Cutlass Supreme
is a wonder of mechanical cannabilism.
Pieces of cars his father's friends share,
junkers that fill backyards and garage space,
disembowelled and doled about.
The tank rolls through the East and North Ends,
faded brown seats and a ride like a great canoe.
In winter the butterfly valve sticks,
the power windows need the help of a pressed hand,
the fan is comically meek
hood up, the engine chuckles phlegmy.

It's a tough old bastard
with a wolf wink
and scummy lips,
chisel point knuckles and ropey arms
cement and exhaust complexion:

An organ of brittle strength
rolling down roads that pimple as they age.

GENERATIONS

Everything returns
to the porch. Our fathers cheering sliding tackles
as theirs in Ireland or Scotland, under pub portraits of the Bruce or Burns
jabbering in yards and garages, blinking around televisions.

K's is best. Poured concrete, like stone cake
hurts your ass if you sit too long. We spit
and drink and smoke
and talk a mile of shit.
Coffees sprout in the grass.

Hangover mornings we find penitence
in singular cures for self-infliction:
from the last of the beer with vitamins
to mismatched grease breakfasts,
scavenged Ibuprofen from someone's medicine cabinet,
or so much water it's drank from brimming pots.

Coffee is the only place we agree.
At night there's a radio, in the day we sit and watch.
We are our fathers,
men who've lost or driven off women
and dreams and haven't thought twice
about things being otherwise.

EVENINGS
Jimmy

We don't even call around most nights.
You just find us at the bar,
still in our steel toes.

The women are so bad even we
don't want them. A whisky silence
chases the beer, and we slump late for cars.

Some of us are all guilt,
never sleeping for regret or fear.

Some are full of blame,
ignorant diatribes made
fierce with liquor and cigarettes.

We all have company
trapped in the solipsism
our mistakes fathered;

dwelling and brooding
for compassion no man can spare.

There is no beauty in this suffering.
We're all broken jazz pianists:
without the redemptive hint of genius.

My loss is like the netting
of dead ivy,
the heaviest debt.

Her absence is innuendo,
what remains after a bat flickers
from nowhere to nowhere.

*

Who's fucking round is it?
Scotty is yelling over the latest chart hit.

What the fuck, Scotty?
It's never your round in your world.

I bought two rounds like three rounds ago.
You bitches got all my money and now you want the rest.

Nick takes his eyes off the girl he's been watching dance.
Pounds twenty dollars onto the bar,
the bartender's cracking caps, calculating.
Four tequilas. She's filling their shots
without watching as she takes the next order,
tosses down the change. Nick pockets it all.

Sissy shit, he says, flicking lemon slices to the floor.

K bangs his shot down and looks to the dance floor.
How come nobody's trying to pick up?
Fuck's wrong with you guys?

Outside in the drizzle,
the crowd hangs out front for a few minutes —
quiet tonight though, no ruckus.

They walk towards the shwarma spot.

Half the seats taken, a lineup at the counter,
Nick watches them shave meat
from the rotating cone. Scotty is bitching,
K and Ronnie listen.

Three guys ahead are fucking around.

The Middle Eastern guys are agitated,
taking orders quickly, saying nothing.

They eat quietly, next to the three loud guys,
who happen to be bigger than Nick thought.

Mac students. Nick looks down at his food.

Nick knows the stare and Scotty's target.
Hey, man. Scotty's eyes shift to meet Nick's.
Easy, hard talker. Nobody's fuck'n around, right?
Scotty chews slowly.
Something small hit's Nick's temple. Onion, tiny and wet.
Both tables tense. The Mac guys are looking at him.
Nick gets his words together. Now, why'd you do that?

Nick sizes up the biggest of the three, but they all grin.
Listen, I ain't look'n for any shit. Been a long week.

The guy is looking more fat than big all at once. Oops, he says.

I think you mean to be saying you're sorry,
know what I mean? Nick cracks his knuckles into place.

The big guy keeps grinning.

I'm gonna say one thing, 'cause you're a big guy
and I don't feel like this. But if we get down,
and the way it's going I don't see how we can't,
I'm gonna fucking mangle you.
I don't know what kind of pussies they got at Mac,
or why your fat ass is thinking you're tough right now,
but I don't give a fuck how much weight you got on me —
I'll fucking kill you.

Everything goes grim. K is smirking
and winks in mock flirt at one of the others.
The big guy doesn't look away
but loses all expression.

He walks out, trailed by his friends.

Thought that was gonna get ugly, guy.
I get a night off from watching Cora
and you've gotta call on the fucking rugby team.

Don't count your chickens. K swallows a mouthful.
I've got a feeling those guys'll find their balls
outside.
                You think he's gonna wait out in that shit?

I hate guys that can't start shit with guys their own size.

K laughs. When was the last time you saw a fair fight?
I saw one in grade two
where there wasn't a third man in
and that was just 'cause nobody was around.

SCOTTY'S

Corktown curries, diapers
and fatigue, desperation
heavy in the stairwell.
Children watch from behind doors
scurry after each other on broken trikes.
At night shouting and laughter poltergeist
the flickering halls.
First of the month brings
two-fours and cartoned smokes —
some canned groceries.
Windows tinfoiled
for the nightshift.

This place is all ears and no ears,
its voice the clip of wire snips,
the muted thump of another bike lock
dropping to the others
around the rusting rail.

UNCLE JOHNNY

I left Helen three years ago January,
galvanized prodigal skipping
back to wasted youth,
from a marriage I believed
stole everything good from my life.
But there is nothing left at forty-seven,
no return for the forsaken.

I returned like a beggar with new eyes
to pubs full of young girls
and found myself inconceivable,
irreconcilable. And everything
I had not even dared to fear
I could be while I lay in bed awake
next to the only woman that would have me,
shuddering to think of having to fuck her.

At first I went alone.
Eager pint of beer in my fist
and dated clothes on my back.
I even saw Nicky out once
and stumbled to him late,
droning drunk about something
expecting to be condoned by his friends.
He was expressionless
when he said in the middle
of what turned into a rant
that he'd see me later.
I slunk off hurt
but not humiliated
till morning.

I later found a guy from work to join me.
We'd talk each other up all day,

like frat guys in the movies.
But we were timid in the bar
and found that sometimes
drunk girls would welcome us
if we approached saying how much
we'd love to buy them a pitcher.
Either they'd guzzle it,
not thank us
and flit off
to varsity boys or (let's face it)
just about anyone,
or their boyfriends would drink most of it
and talk to us, hurting us worse with pity.

We roped a couple in.
When you're out every other night
it's bound to happen.
Shy or polite girls,
or ones who just couldn't fathom
that men our age could be after them.
A couple of slurring, ambitious compliments
usually cured that,
though one of us might
separate a cagey nymph from the group
the booze told us
would be willing if we could only
keep her listening
to the rambling praise.
More beers only convinced us
of our comfort with them,
the effortless brilliance of our cajoling
though they'd edge metres between us
in cushioned booths,
finger watches at each other,

gesture with eyebrows
in terms so indiscreet
that even we would notice.

He and I left together,
despondent in the backs of cabs
through empty streets past houses
filled with families and men
we could not help but imagine
in our desolation
had made the right choices.
Men we had pretended to feel sorry for.

HELEN

When you left
I cleared your garden
grew bulbing blisters
through thin gloves
and the claw
of a garden tool sparkled
in my hand like a weapon.

The garden fought back.
Every last root forced me
to mercilessness —
arm-plucked like spines
freed with earth and rocks
like wormy hearts
to bake dead in the sun.

I tore up your garden and paved it.
Poured asphalt into the wounds
then crushed the surface smooth.

It's black behind the house now,
my victory
paved beneath.

NORTH END AUBADE

The harsh bleep of the alarm clock
is the fear we take to bed.

Fear of midnight pisses,
that sleep will not grapple
us, and we will lay awake
in frantic exhaustion.

Watch dawn inch
maliciously towards us,
churn reticent knowing skies.

★

Every morning I fight my way
from bed to breakfast
then pause when tying my boots.
There's a moment where the day
before me is a prison sentence
to be endured with the same look
my father's grown into over the years.

I used to think of work when I wasn't there.
For the first few months it stole all my time.
I fight the nausea in the morning,
the dread of going
and try not to think of it
until I'm in.

A teacher once told me about a poet who said work
was like a big toad squatting on you.

Not for me.

Work's a tapeworm
taking what little you get
hungrily, with you everywhere
maliciously feeding,
lining eyes, stooping posture,
eating eating eating
till you're just a husk.

STONE

The stone of work is the weight
of running out the clock.
Nick leaves his watch in his pocket —
it's hell to look at the time every two minutes.
He's learning to forget the clock
wishing his life away.
Busy hands are the only way
to make the day go.

When shift bell sounds quitting time
Nick steps into the hot wall of air
off the asphalt lot.
Clicks open his bike lock
pedals like a released prisoner
intent on making up what is lost.
He races transports on Burlington Street,
feet sore in steel-toes, lungs like hot pillows.

Chad is bleary-eyed on the porch; with two girls
in heavy makeup who watch Nick like dolls.
Chad reaches down to stub the roach.
Whadup?
Just work, guy, Nick says,
his thoughts beyond here,
ever on what is coming.

RICKY

Uncle Rick's a roofer
his life is draining cases
hammering nails in the bleaching sun
bursting noses in bar fights

a two packs a day guy
you could strike a match on his knuckles

old friends turned bikers
call with work
pay in kilos that line a cupboard
he sells but never smokes
disappears into strip club back rooms
with shoulder-clapping full-patch members

Rick is a great belly, huge fists
an alcoholic laugh and complacence

life to him is a great crude joke

two-fours are a business expense
his days are extra large coffees
in the blazing mornings
beers and a comically tiny sandwich at noon
fries and the better end of a case
packing up gear and expertly careening
the crusting van through twilight
backstreets home.

KITCHEN SINK
Ricky

Miserable bastards alone together
lined up at the bar and staring into their bottles
like psychic spoon-benders,
or talking endless earnest garbage, destitute therapy.
Bitch drunk or nearly crying about ex-wives,
estranged children, bosses, losses.
Hard-nosed cowards skirting the loneliness
that really kills every single one of us.
We don't even have conversations;
we get drunk and one-way the guy next to us
or he gets there first and spills.
A scrap is the only way out.
It's welcome, therapy too,
and then it's an ugly old-man fight.
Just bare-bones stuff,
none of that shuffling, feinting bullshit;
young men think it's a fucking boxing match.

Want some advice?
I been in enough bar fights
to tell you throw the full fucking arsenal
especially if you're a broken down palooka.
Kitchen-sink the fucker and get it over with.
And don't worry too much when you see him next time,
he needed that, just like you.

HANGOVER
Ricky

woke up starwise on the front lawn
a whisky-crooked asterisk
terrible new world of cold and bright and sound
like rising from a warm bath

grass dry and dirt a crust against my body
throat like a scab

the flawless sky overbright
and I laboured onto my stomach

heard my neighbour's car
the creak and bang of screen doors
gravel-grate of steps on the sidewalk

I breathed deep so they'd see I was alive
and leave me alone

that's all I have strength to ask for these days
alone in the bar or my living room
alone in the coloured dark of my closed eyes

still drunk I mumbled fuck it
and slept the whole day in the sun

BARTON BUS

Nick watches inside and out
using his twelve for an armrest.

An old lady with a pen
embroiders Chinese characters
onto a wrinkling page.

Hunter-gatherers
in ten-month beards
jostle trashcans for bottles;
daily traplines.

The hospital hulks past
and pauses for a father
and son to board and sit.

Windows move the world again —
an arm falls like a gaunt, tattooed wing
around teenage shoulders;
the father leans in and whispers,
We stay in this scrap.

RONNIE AT WORK

In a dungeon of shivering machines
Ronnie pulls the plate
executioner's mask
from his drenched face
and lowers the momentarily
calmed torch.

Richest and poorest of the boys,
a full tradesman with a white flame
in the bowels of the steel mill,
his father, Ronan,
is a barking foreman
at home as well.
Ronnie gulps down
half the water he carries
everywhere, refilling
the bottle several
times a day,
losing much of it
to the work.

In the deep hum and hot dark
he swears through Catholic teeth
at the irony of finding peace
in a place so much like hell.

When not welding, he's never without coffee.
He stays up half the night
trying not to go to bed with Jen
who goes to bed as early as possible
for the same reason.
They rotate together,
share a couple's dream of shift work —
and their own nightmare.

Unhappy almost from the beginning,
they live together
in the basement apartment
below his parents.

His daughter Cora
is the only woman he's sure
he will ever love.

Ronan punishes Ronnie for this.
Ronnie spends as much time
alone with Cora as he can.

His only other peace is here:
a job finished, fifteen minutes to spare
in the loud heat
and a little water.

BLOW

Deep in a ring of light pressed
on all impossible sides
by attentive silence,
we weight and cut
a chalky fortune
scraped about rough
like it were just dust
our menace focused
speechless

eyes everywhere.

At two we chase a scrawny line
with black coffee,
and then back to the razor's
merry malice —

the misery
I carve
innocent in little
grinning piles

★

She blows three good puffs
blinks wide, then it's blood rushing
in her ears like wind.

★

Sprawled on her double mattress
pane keeping out the city
morning ruckus and cold.
A morning she discovered

in grey bloom
as she stepped from the basement
and hailed a cab
and scratched in the back seat.

He won't call.
She knows
all the machinery of the city
will move without her,
languish with all
she's brought to herself.

There will be no relief from arms
she'd give three pints of blood
to sleep safe in.
He will never call.

She wishes for dreams of warmer places —
where love might not be so fucked
so painful, so wrong —
but she cannot even dream of warm rain.

CARLA

When the ugly-lights come up
they're all out, furious young men
in collared shirts stinking
of drugstore cologne.
This isn't escapism sex
in these Thursday night cheap drink bars,
this is all small egos and fuck-hunger,
the sad need to feel that women
will claw their way across dance floors
dying to go home and ravage you.

Some juice-bag is raging across the street,
his friends trying to calm him
when a car of guys pulls up
and next they're shredding shirts —
it disperses as quickly as it started
and the juice-bag is still raging,
only bleeding a bit now.

Kasia and I sit and eat hotdogs
watch a spotlight trace the ceiling of night,
pretending the city is alive.

Two guys passing,
one cussing drunk about how he hates his girl
for her anthology of men,
a girl abused by issues.
"Nobody wants to think
about a bunch of guys
doing that to their girl."

It's empty now and all for show
we pass two other girls
on our way to catch a cab on King,

one pretends not to see the pack
stare her up and down.
Her friend is on a cell
skin smoothed with streetlight
saying, I love you too, baby.
I'll be home soon.

FRIDAY

Off to hear a band on Friday night
the shiver of a cymbal at the door,
ink-sleeved bouncer, bored
turning ogre shoulders
to survey a room that's seated or propping a wall.
The boys shuffle past the boulder of his belly
single file through the crowd
for the nicked finish of the bar.
The sallow barmaid who turns for
K's order is pregnant.

The band caterwauls,
cougars dance awkwardly up close.
Hey, Ronnie! K hollers,
bet even you could bag one of those!

They shoot a round of rye
and take their beers to the side.
The band breaks down for the next act.

They rest their beers on a ledge and settle.
A solitary girl gets on stage,
rests two guitars near a stool,
shies eyes, sets everything in place.
In a fast slink she is off to a group of girlfriends.
A round of shots in unison
and she whisks back up again.
I'd bend that over, Scotty loudly allows.
Round, boys, Nick moves through the crowd's ebb and sway.
He plants an elbow and leans a shoulder in,
bill folded in his fingers. He turns
at the same moment as the girl next to him,
and manages a reflexive, Hey.

DOWN AT THE KICK'N STAB

The doorman is descended from hangmen,
an ancient English cruelty finds kinship
in the torturous reach of his fingers.
He delights in havoc, the quickening of violence
and horror for duty, God,
or some other descendent hoax.
He's a mastiff, snarling to be released.
A Celtic cross scars his steroid-plump bicep,
dullness a disguise for ravenous hate.

The barmaid is fearsome.
She's gone twelve rounds with cocaine and crack —
her bout with liquor will end when one of them dies.
Her daughter is in juvie for something grizzly —
beating fresh girls as they come in —
she still can't make the pain go away.
Her husband sailed off the mountain brow
in a rusting car, a singing dove drunk
and enamoured by the moon, down down down
into the city beneath where flames floated up.

The busboy is forty, disabled
after taking every drug he could,
lives now in the slow world of inhalants.
A puckering scar slithers from his left ear
to his right collarbone.
He has spells of confusion,
wakes in the middle of conversations,
walks staring at his toes,
recites key-chain affirmations at the bus stop,
clutching exact change.

BARTON AND KENILWORTH RAMBLE

Centre of the city is where I'm at.
I squabble my best friend for a fuck'n quarter
and scream over nickels on a bill.
When I've been in the rye
I don't give a fuck for fighting,
Hell, I'll whittle your down cheeks with this bottle.
Don't pretend when you talk.
You're no better'n me.
Don't look at me like you've never hit your woman.
I've crushed a roll of quarters in my fist
scattered their wits and teeth.
And fuck you. Fuck you.
I was born here
and nobody's feeling good
when I'm not.

Fuck, I never get this drunk. If I had a revolver
this'd be the worst night the North End's ever seen.
I'd shoot my friend for playing broke,
that waitress for being bucktoothed,
and the bartender for looking on.

The street's rocking
and quieter than my ears.
I'm so fuck'n numb
even this sidewalk at my cheek
is too gentle.

*

Strength ebbed from labour and liquor,
the Saturday morning coffee trudge is slow torment.
Nick and K lumber humid streets
for the coffee shop on Barton.

Jen surprises them at the counter —
hadn't anticipated her
though Ronnie had warned them.

They reach her like an angry finish line.

Two coffees, Jen, K says.
They hate each other openly
for Ronnie.

Hear Cora's getting big, Nick says, too sweet.
Jen scrutinizes. Ronnie never stops talking
about his girl. Jen softens a little
and gives them their coffee.
What'd you guys do last night?

Ate pizza and did each other's nails...

Nick cuts K off — Ronnie needs to get out
and he never drinks all that much.
He knows and we know you don't like it,
but he's not doing it to hurt you.

She hates me, K says outside.
Think? Why you gotta be so hard on her?
Please, that girl was meant to ruin some poor guy's life —
I just try to make her feel shitty while she's at it.

OLD-TIME CHAMP
Lincoln

I'm an old-time champ, baby.
I throw bags of concrete all day
and box my busted hands all night.
I'll spar two hours solid
and never even hit a bag
for months.

My body shots'll make you shit in your shoes.
I'm made of harder stuff than you.
I was born scrapp'n.
It's my natural state
so I don't even have to win
but, bitch, when I want to
I can spin some cheetah shit,
phantom flicker 'round your range
and stagger you at will.

I get a first taste of everybody.
You come in here
like a baby elephant on a big fuck'n chain,
but no matter how big you grow
I can still lead you around
because I see what your instincts are.
You come in here
and hit the pads,
you hit the bag a while and then I come up
out of nowhere when you look
like your balls are growing and drop my word.
Nobody's got the guts to say no,
and I never throw a punch in that first round
but I don't let you land any either;
that's the only lesson you'll get from me.
I start hitting a bit in the second
and we go from there.

I run here after a work day you couldn't take,
I take Macfarlane apart
and that kid'll break your little bitch ass in half.
I got a girl that don't care about how great I am in here,
a mom who needs a third of my cheque,
cousins with gold teeth you'd be scared to know.
People come in here and pretend it's pride and glory.
Pride and glory are luxuries.
Only rich people believe in that shit.

*

Nick and Carla have talked
three times on the phone.

Muscular in the underwater
dark of her room,
rubbing lotion
into chlorine-starched shoulders,
a nakedness she never tells him about.

He beached
after a day in the hot slither
his work clothes hardening dry
on the back of a chair.

They'll share a late lunch on a Saturday
at her place by the university.
Nick tells K and the guys at work but not his father.
He thinks about her at the gym
and on his ride to work,
and isn't sure he remembers what she looks like.

Carla is from the country, from Alliston.
Filling Nick's head with fecundity
encouraging his belief
that she's a different, finer creature.
Everything she reveals delights him.

The poetry of her —
spaces between words and times
he can fill with something growing.

CARLA

She walks like a panther,
water-polo back and shoulders rippling.
She splits books on finance
on a student ghetto porch, ignoring the landlord
neighbour who farts through a trombone.
She wears only sandals when it's warm,
even to bars, and always walks
with wet hair and a gym bag.
Like most varsity girls
she drinks infrequently
and only to get drunk
and is watched everywhere.

She sleeps in an old Nationals T-shirt,
eats pasta for breakfast and Müslix for dinner.
She watches the news and her one sitcom.
She is businesslike at her studies,
rolls her eyes at girls
with expensive purses
and aristocratic migraines.
She is sprung from solid earth
as much as from her own mother
and knows this to her core.

TWO ROOMS

Carla rents a one-storey with Kasia —
they sublet to a docile exchange student
they rarely see or hear.
Kasia listens to indie rock and emo writing papers,
slim joint clenched in her teeth,
Chinese Boading balls cycling in her free hand.
Kasia is a frenetic miracle.
There are notes and library books in her food cupboard.
Her guitar a derelect,
lazy guest on the couch.
There's a small jungle at her window,
postcards, socialist icons, Eastern trinkets,
and a directionless library
of Sutras, American history, symbolic logic —
half-poems or song lyrics scrawled
on napkins, cans of organic beans
stacked in the closet.

Carla's room is messier
aiming at order.
She has five pairs of battered runners,
sports bras and speedos draped everywhere,
text ziggurats, notes squeezing out.
There are pictures of her father's farm,
her family, herself hiking in Alberta.
She's the more solid creature;
Kasia is scent and ether,
a ghost of clues and warnings.

AFTER LUNCH IN THE MAC GHETTO

There is a different kind of poverty here —
the proud novelty of doing without
until tomorrow.

All North-End biceps and lines
around his eyes darkening, Nick sits
watching white guys in dreadlocks
across the street. On their balcony
they grow pot, and think spirituality's,
Carla says, chai tea and Tai Chi.
Nick snickers, not sure he really gets it,
though he catches the gist.

Everyone here looks like they dye their hair and jog.
It's halfway to what Nick imagines California,
blond hair, Rollerblades
and hiking shorts everywhere.

Kasia on the phone —
"narratives" and "dialectic" — intimidates him,
though he knows some words
are for just that.
Carla stalks with two mugs
of black coffee and sits heavily
on the other second-hand lawn chair.
She winks an eye as brown as polished oak,
and takes a searching sip.
Nick cracks his neck comfortably.
Carla reaches out to curl short-nailed fingers
around his bicep. I like you, Macfarlane, she says,
and kisses him softly before the coffee reaches his lips.

SATURDAY NIGHT AGAIN

Weaving home with the tracks
dawn meek in the chameleon sky
growing from the horizon of his shoulders
Nick sits drunk between the rails
looking way down into their oblivion.
He can suddenly feel them out there
conducted through the steel:

other places and lives of his own.

Nick has seen Toronto, but lately his dreams
are of Kingston, Edmonton, Sacramento.

A strange moment of feeling snared,
the tracks a patient V to everywhere
and everything else he could be.

*

Talking with her creates new landscapes in him.

A muscular childhood outside Alliston
under every kind of sky imaginable.

A wholly different kind of work
that does not end with the clock
but does not haunt you.

Tangled fields beneath slate sky in autumn,
earth soft after rain, hard and sharp as cracked ice in winter,
a distance the city has no words for.

Brick house from another time.
Nodding orchards live and die and live again.
Still brood and bloom of the fields and sky
and he and Carla together
in new myths of northern emptiness.

KNOCKOUT

Lincoln gets riled when you clip his ears,
and I was grinding them for a cauliflower
and giving him nasty hooks to the ribs
when he tried to protect them.
I stomped his toes once on purpose,
slipped most of what he threw at me,
and whispered in his ear when we got close.

I didn't feel the punch,
just the detachment.

Time disengaged;
the drop
slow and gentle.

Canvas like a wall
I was pushed against.

I sprawl, pinned by the lights,
encased in the heavy air
that holds my thrashing still.

CORNER STORE

The man at the corner store
lives in a rented basement
a few blocks away
and labours home smoking
every night, depleted,
getting fat and old
at an amazing rate.
He's learned to bellow
to scare shoplifting kids,
to greet old men
with cigarettes ready,
to forget his inventory
so he must rise and leave
the whispering TV
to rustle chips
or reach into a thicket
of pop — he's learned sanity
is in the imagination
of other lives
as they swoop
through and pay.

BARTON BUS
Ronnie

The thing about the bus is that it's depressing,
a small room in the vein of our associated lives,
everyone pushed or pulled and consumed.

I'm so sick about money
that I've forgotten the symptoms:
I wade about our cramped place
to make a point in the fight
Jen and I have fought
since the beginning.

It's a mild nausea,
a nervous gut really,
like hot tea after cayenne pepper.

My eyes,
not bleary, but spent,
tell her —
he's wearing down nicely.

CANDLESTICK KID
Jimmy

I was the worst boxer in the world
for ten years because of my father,
the Candlestick Kid:

> "One blow to the head and he's gone."

I broke my nose and my jaw trying to win
his whisky-stinking love.
Bought me a pair of second-hand gloves
took me to gyms that wouldn't even admit girls
where I stumbled over new drills
in my exhausted size sevens. Ignored
me when I'd done well, or listened bored.
Gave me a look when I lost that was worse
than disappointment because after a tough spar
they said, "I was expecting that, you silly little shit.
You'll never be a man. You haven't got it
in you." He only ever gave a nod to the older boys,
gliding grown between the ropes,
winning their sixteenth fights, not slumping home
to the voice of their fathers, like cold, heavy stone.

JIMMY

My life's pastimes:
work and off hours spent depressed
about the other's approach.

I've become the guy at work who never laughs,
who really only hates
himself; the father who's given up fathering

except for when I'm drunk
— but not caved in —
and I have to sit and listen to myself
ramble forty steady minutes of shit
to Chad or Nick,

or sit on the bus and let the young guys see
what they never want to become.

THE SHADOW OF A COIN
Jimmy

When the jewel in the wrinkled mouth
slipped for me, I discovered there is nothing
but obligation.

Two boys and the monthly envelopes,
a slack fatherhood that cannot find another way

The violent loneliness I feared when I was young,
everything I worried about...

I feel like the raccoon I watched
scramble a tree
the height of a house
and fall,
claws skittering, thumping blind
to the ground that raced to meet it.

Rabid with shock and terror
wheeling in rings with a leg that looked broken,
it clattered up
and fell again.

It struck its spine square on the chain-link,
a slapstick terror, then two more tries
before it could no longer remain conscious:

curled, bleeding
against the fence
until nightfall
when it could see
and escape.

At best what I am feels like the shadow cast by a flipped coin.

Now only finds you when it's four hours to go to bed and the
cable goes —
Now only finds you when I'm late for work and the engine
won't turn —
Now only finds you when you close the shoebox of your wedding
pictures —
And feel like a monster for not being able to muster a breath for
Stay with me.

FRAGILE
Ricky

My mind is a fume within the ceramic of my skull

whisky depression settles over the guy next to me
singing someone else's sad songs

the scarred drink as an excuse
to pound migraines into each other

when you drink the whispers
only become sharper and crueller

I don't taste the sea or the Ganges
or the fucking morning dew

this is a glass of cold symptoms
the polluted harbour

fragility

GREED
Ricky

Archie hollers
for a fresh pitcher
through the wired jaw
he was well enough
to break scrapping.
He's been drunk
in a back brace
since the accident,
and laughs
because his comp
will hold till
he gets disability.

He's jaundiced
from the whisky
painkiller cocktail,
his eyes orangey
horrors. He smirks
like a lottery winner:
his shit basement place
and can-of-tomato-soup dinners
and beers all day
accounted for
as long as
he's careful.

There's just one sin in this world
he says, pouring me a half pint,

greed.

THREE WEEKS
Carla

Nick grinds his bike to my place
after boxing
even when he's worked all day.
We curl up on my couch
with the TV on in the background
and just talk. We'll doze a little
then he'll put me to bed
and bike home
and never even complain
when he calls the next day
that he was tired at work.

LAND
Carla

My textbook falls to my chest
and I dream the tall cathedrals of economics.
The clergy feverish in packs
white collars and coats like gowns
in wind-filled prism corridors.

Virtue and sin are invented again.
Noble and ignoble crushed or embellished
for a real salvation.

My grandfather acquired our farm
in the Calvinism of the stock market.
In the ritual of prayer and study,
labyrinth of indices traversed in faith,
watched theocracy come to pass.
And by grace he was delivered
to a literal promised land.

FAMISHED
Carla

My first trip out
to a Hamilton I haven't seen before.

Kids pedal pigeon-toed single file up driveways
to huge men bear-laughing on their porches
fists sprouting the necks of beers
caps seeding their unplanted gardens
talk of alimony hockey shot clutches and assholes on comp.
Nick laughs; the North End is performing.

This barroom table feels like lacquer drying
clinging the fine hairs on my forearms.

Nick leans across
his unshaven face
rough to my fingers
eyes like a lynx flash the room
take me in at a glance.

Men have wanted me before
but this is different.
Nick is famished for me.
A confident present restraint —
until the minute we're outside.

I'll grind his back
into the crab grass in the park
swim hard over him
drown him in me.

ROUTINE

He has ached himself from her
to a drained two-wheeled totter
through the unsleeping
student ghetto, then the miles
of sleeping houses
back to a North End
that is half asleep
and half raging
itself broken
into the night.

Bed is a dark flash
then the alarm clock
across the room.

Morning passes
a foot behind his eyes
thick lens of exhaustion
forcing the world
to a distance
that will not be recovered
until he naps before boxing and returns to Carla's bed.

*

She's with me everywhere now —
the warehouse or dreamless sleep

tapping feeling inside my head
like a seashell she's found

running fingers across its grooves
learning smooth and ridged sides

fingernail click acoustics
this is what it feels like

every moment
her making me hers.

KASIA'S OPEN MIC NIGHT POEM

I'd like to remind you that while I'm a grad student on coffee
    and caffeine pills,
You're a horrid old bat who's nicer to strangers than her family.

And though it's true that I'm an armchair socialist,
You're a compassionless hawk who lets the cold-war propaganda
    of sitcoms form your political beliefs.

And yes, while I flaunt my gay lovers and gossip loudly about
    sexual escapades in restaurants,
You're a mild young crank who'd rather stay in and make lentil
    soup than rave and rage in chemical euphoria.

And sure, I do drink too much and I'm late with my ringer off,
But you're a coked-up asshole at a party with a complex that
    none of his friends are genuine and no one will miss him.

And though I'm the first to admit that I say "cock" too often,
You're an asexual bitch who wields the sex she could have like a
    cudgel.

In fact, you're:

An asshole jock bartender in a ball cap playing hip-hop in a pub
A pretentious chick in square-rim glasses half drunk at a party
    yapping about Derrida
An undergraduate who plays video games all semester and takes
    Ritalin for exams
A rich girl bitching about her summer job
A guy with no guts trying to edge his way into line at the bus
    station
An old lady snipping that it's cruel to let the homeless have dogs
An old man who actually believes being gay is a choice

A vegan who always has a cold and never tires of nagging the rest of us

A girl who sleeps with guys to get over other guys that didn't want her either

A nineteen-year-old in the bar washroom shrieking hatefully about how horny he is

A rich guy who thinks that he really could be happy if he just cheated on his wife

A woman who thinks emotional austerity and criticism are motherhood

A father who chose the bottle

A kid with plans to frame her teacher as a pedophile — as a joke

A criminal's wet dream — bitching about the cops and driving drunk

A teenager who picks on the kid who just lost his father

An elementary school princess who bullies the quiet girl

A miserable fat guy with road-rage

A suburban family who bought a big house just to flee each other

A person who creates his own, and others' misery and doesn't know it.

Every last fucking one of you.

IN CARLA'S BEDROOM

All night the conspiracy of talk
of childhoods and preferences
of school days and futures
of movies and music
of the all-important trivialities

Slick with moisturizers
Carla is a full-bodied miracle
round hips and soft muscular stomach

Her body curving; an ellipse
that Nick's fingers trace endlessly
following following to no end

As her sleep deepens she winds
her fingers into his

They are everywhere gently knotting

LOVE AND QUIESCENCE
Carla

It really can only be these tiny things

that still moment before you're aware of me
when I come upon you in the kitchen
filled with morning, your hand
arranging cheeses and greens for the both of us

when you leave everything for that instant

reaching gently across the mattress for my cheek
as though I am new and sudden
barely real and yours.

You go silent when we walk
and your hand — mistaken
by passersby as instinct —
slips softly into mine.

*

Carla

summer classes
and training
and nights curled up
whispering
for him to stay
though he never does

Nick phantoms
past my window
while I lay
in the hot space
he has left

and spread myself

*

Home late

sweat everywhere from the bike
and exhaustion behind eyes like soft weight
Nick finds Ricky sprawled across the couch
drinking with his father.
Work in five hours.

Up late, Nicky.
Tobacco rich laugh
and an ice-tinkling glass raising
to Rick's lips.
Get laid for your birthday?

Isn't my birthday.

Then our little Nicky's growin' up.

Drunken snicker;
Rick's joke buried somewhere.

Not worried about work in the morning?
Nick flicks his chin at the empty whisky bottle.

Fuck it, Nick.
Neither of us got anything worth waking up for.

Nick looks at his feet for a second. Yeah.
Labours a numb flight of stairs underfoot
then an empty instant of sleep.

*

Kasia

I was at a kegger last night
wearing a shirt that said
"I know an army of poetic socialists
but have never met a scientific one"
and this boy comes up
like it's the shirt he wants to talk about
so I told him Philosophy was like
a bunch of men laying on rafts on a lake
reaching down,
unable to see bottom;
some have slightly longer arms
but the bottom simply can't be reached this way
and that's all there is to it

When he tried to kiss me
I lied and said I only like girls
and he not only bought it
he said it was great and went away

Sometimes I just don't get these guys

CARLA'S JOURNAL

I'm falling for you, Macfarlane.
Come away with me into the sleeping places;
I'll show you the earth I grew strong in.

I'm lovely and sweet and fierce
and I'll change your life.

Let me begin with this.
Let me sweep you north,
show you new sky
and new fields to run,

walk the world
next to me.

HIS
Jen

I wake before Ronnie every morning.
Almost a game, the race
to see if I can get so far ahead in my routine
that I won't need to speak to him before I leave.

But I can never escape his father,
always upstairs, elbows holding down the table
drinking his black breakfast.
I suspect he spends the night there.
Ronan never says a word, just watches me.
I imagine he does the same to Ronnie.

I walk to work, an over-romanticized idea, let me tell you.
Late night is the worst shift. All the men with open sores
and wired jaws, Tourette's ticks, or so low with calamity
that when they struggle the coffee to their lips
it actually seems to take a sip from them.

Morning shifts are a rush of contractor vans,
talk of tool theft, moonlighting and contract gossip,
everyone happy to see me, vaguely acknowledging need.
I spill cups full and fling sandwiches
that come from somewhere else,
someone would know, I don't, and donuts
the baker has puffed from little rings.

I'm all smiles and flirtation here.

I eat little and stand as much as I can,
keep my makeup flawless to spite Ronnie.
I stay lithe and sharp,
though we'll probably never have sex again.
I comb my raven hair to princess smoothness,
rub the legs I've just scraped

clean with a razor, flash my eyes at the mirror,
showing him what will never be his again.

We've cost each other so much,
all we share now is our vital hate.

NIGHT SHIFT AT THE COFFEE SHOP
Jen

Is an old man
twisting his toque in his hands
before a cold and untouched cup

A pock-scarred teenager
shivering feverishly in her sweater
despite the summer heat

A middle-aged man
plunking the same quarter
in the pay phone and waiting out
the agony of ring after unanswered ring

Gang flags
leaning close across the table
obvious in their whispers

A hare-lipped woman
ticking
and switching seats
muttering at her reflection
in the black mirrors
night has made of the windows

Men with suspiciously shaved heads
and gym bags and ink-sleeved forearms
that could crack my bones like meringue
waiting for cellphones to ring

★

Never a moment alone
though loneliness is the rule

★

Guards from Barton talking
about jail's cautious clockwork

Police place orders
with gentle regret and sit
for five minutes in the parking lot

City nightworkers smiling
truck panting in the lot
thinking the bitter pornography
of men surrounded by men

★

And all the good mothers in their beds
in houses with lush lawns
in suburbs that stretch silent miles
and their soulmates sleeping soundly next to them

make me want to put a sugar jar through the window

ICE

Vigilant, unwavering
the camera in the police cruiser
watches the kid clamber madly in
crank the column with a screwdriver

mouth blasting
digits poking
at the radio dashboard speedometer
eyes hands berserk
teeth gnashing
skeleton trying to escape skin
muscles tendons revolting
explosion of tense insanity
frenetic torture
screaming faster faster *faster*

the ambulance driver
who finds the kid still twitching
after the crash
asks later in desolate gravity
to see the recording

to see what that bulling heart
and strength looked like
the unconscious maniac grip
that almost broke his hand

to see hell
in the windless howls
on the screen

APPROACH

The guys at work talk about the long weekend
like three days off is forever.
Camping with their step-children
or real children that divorced wives have taken
or doing light carpentry on cottages or houses alone.
They expect me to go on a three-day bender —
the working man's dream.

I tell them Carla is taking me
to meet her family.

It's weird to see a bunch of guys
too scared to congratulate
and too confused to joke —
somewhere in it all
there's something that makes them a little happy
and really, really jealous.

TO ALLISTON

There is a rhythm the borrowed car finds
in the gravel concession road's subtle lurching.
Carla steers from her muscular shoulder,
arm straight out as if guiding a bus or tractor
not a four cylinder bucket with suspicious flooring.
She rests a massive coffee against her crotch
and stares into the distance, confident as a prizefighter.

The morning is bright
and Carla's sunglasses
hold the same white spark
that rolls up passing windshields.

Nick feels he's in a borrowed place.

Who planted endless telephone poles?
The infinity of roadside reflectors?

Old women pat loam around geraniums
in halved barrels converted to roadside flower pots.
Children skirt machine-groomed cornfields.
Men laugh beneath truck hoods and toss parts
into the grass growing around their ankles.

Nick will find himself alive with this.
He will close his eyes and see plumed cornstalks
fluttering in the night. For now the sun
reflects off the leaves like a harbour,
casting, striking a line to the tousling sky.

STORM ACROSS CORNFIELDS
Carla

Tonight a Virgilian wind tremored
from trunk to branch
and the rain shivered
applause from the corn.

Sudden fluorescence
strobes shadows
split unnaturally
and leave us
in an utter black,
nature snapping the chain
of its cousin from our sockets.

Crocuses of flame spring from candles.

The room flashes
into and out of existence
stranding me in the squeeze
of this bucking, heaving
world of you.

COUNTRY NIGHT

Nick wades the dark hallway
for the washroom, senses alive
to new air, new quiet,
everything here, from the tapwater
to the darkness, is richer
clean and organic
everything sighing

the panting of Carla's dog eases
from downstairs

through the hall window, field and sky

Carla is behind him a moment later
chin on his shoulder
soft earth of her in his nostrils
arms reaching around him crisscross
pulling his square chest with both hands:

they stand watching
the storm has made indeterminate
the place where earth meets sky

NICK IN ALLISTON

After six eggs and a pint of coffee each,
Carla and her father leave Nick to explore
the still bristle of country morning.

On the porch that wraps the house
Nick stands a long time
watching sunlight move.

He steps off
and walks to the edge
of a turned field
as though it is a lake
follows a kitten into a chicken coup
filled with straw and wild cats
that hiss him out the way he came.

Carla's younger brother is at the far end of the barn
spinning on a concrete pad and hurling a steel ball
comically short distances out the great open doors.

Steven smiles; burly even in his cheeks.
He offers Nick the chalky shot.
It is not heavy
until he thinks about throwing it.
Compelled by the challenge
Nick hefts it an arm's length above his head,
groans the stubborn thing out
and watches it pull itself down hard to the earth
like a thing that meant to humiliate
and had an easy time of it.

THROWING
Steven

Dad and I built the circle
in the south end of the barn
and I throw from it

quiet cannonading
into long grass every afternoon
until the snow settles.

I snug that steel bud into my neck,
tap my toes on the concrete twice and spin out,
launching her long into my dad's
Send her for a ride, Steve!

The coyotes cheer in their own way
and the rabbits watch
and no one understands my strength.

I lift engines and push the carcasses of cars
my dad leaves about for parts;
I heave bits of the Canadian shield about
when they bob from the fields looking for air and light.
I pull free burgeons of stone
and heft them up
as far as they've ever been from earth.

We drive the shuddering truck out to meets
May through August,
and I throw in noon-bright fields
against tall city kids with ropy muscles and mean glares.

No one can touch the meditation of my spin,
I merely send the shot,
though all they see are heavy legs,

the boughs of my biceps,
the flash flicker of my dense wrist.

FARM
Carla

Where glaring February mornings
make the barn a dark cavern,
the summer glows everywhere
with the frozen brightness
of January in Montreal
(without the red wine
and bikes and twisted staircases).
Real Ontario cicadas fill the night in July
as the breeze flutters the crowds of field.
From the porch life is a still carnival.
August makes the wide sky wisp
or unfurls the bank of a thunderstorm.
September rain makes trees and cornfields clap.
This is the extent of our animation.
Here we are the calmest people.

*

Jen

The night I told Ronnie about it
I was a wreck.

We'd been together two months
and he was visiting my family
up by Kingston
and everything
was a new dream.

He studied the sidewalk
then looked through it
and said that a good man
would only consider the best way
and that he would be my man
and a father to the child
and I swear I burst
the hottest tears
as my terrified body relaxed.

On the way home,
bus barrelling
between the night fields
and sleeping places,
a child two rows ahead started to cry.

It was loud and turned to gasping
and spluttering and went on and on.
Ronnie and I sat in the dark,
hearts too afraid to thrash,
letting the bus hurtle us
straight ahead, our hands frozen
in each other's laps
and the world outside
passing us.

*

Ronan   .

The rain like poured nails
on the shed where I'm drinking
and fixing the mower
and meditating
to the mad snare.

This is the weather my father
said made him
homesick.

Through the door I can watch
the drops fall
like needles
into the lawn.

BECOME
Carla

I mutter first, snarling
staring a mile
through the change room wall
or mirror or the murmuring stands
and I feel my billowing self harden:

I am born sharp-eyed and reptilian.

On land my muscles relax
into a soft life.

Water galvanizes,
the dense liquid I become
sinister and overwhelming.

Before you become water you fear it
slap through gasping
sure only of its smothering logic.
But you can depend on water,
and I become
part of its remorseless consistency.

MARRIAGE
Ronnie

I learned marriage from my father
though I'm not married.

When you're with someone you hate
you accept and forget
to stay sane.

I breathe in the cramped spaces of work,
spend nights ignoring everything
that isn't Cora,

and wondering
how this could ever work
or why people say it will.

SEWING

Lincoln almost never hits the bag,
but when he does he peppers
the uncanny rhythm of an old sewing machine,
a preposterous papapopping
dancing and papapapapapopping again.
Fists quick threading
darning and sewing into the leather,
feet easing up and down
as he pedals his weight
to adjust speed and power.
"Hey, Macfarlane," he yells,
"Wanna get sewn?"

COLT
Ronan

My life is the sum of the things I've gathered as my own.
The earwig colony of a shed more rust than paint,
this ragged lawn, a son who cares nothing for Irish roots
and brings a brat and brat-mother under my blighted roof,
tattered bed lamp Bible,
the battered ring my grandfather gave me
when I left Limerick as a boy.

The only thing I have that's
dream-bright is the Colt
locked up in the basement.
I think sometimes about how I could
sit with it in the kitchen
snipe tiny holes in my back door
plug the whole frame out if I wanted,
how it would lean and fall stiffer than a body
if I hit the right places,
how I could go into the streets
with my pockets full of ammo
and shoot streetlights
to see them shatter.

I could pop out every one —
even the cop sirens spinning
as they barricade
and blast me into
a nearly painless blink.
But a man has his burdens,
and you do not do these things.

You do not do these things.

WARM UP AT SCOTTY'S
K

Twelves clink behind us at arm's length
each already one short
as we walk to Scotty's
where neighbours narrow through doors
and it's all curries and cornrows
and we never see the dads —
like these kids have the opposite problems as us.
The television is never off
only neglected —
spins muted infomercials
shows about gardening
or celebrity cars —
the scent of hours-old hash always in the air.
Scotty eats shit, even for one of us.
Sometimes we huddle at the table
twelves under our seats
(we're all scared of his fridge)
and laugh at the tin mounds
or microwave packaging
heaping in his garbage
and leaking across his counter.
Past tenants smoked walls sticky
the toilet is something
a hobo wouldn't sit on,
we call the balcony the raccoon nest.

We can hear the neighbour
fucking through the wall
and he can hear us laughing.

*

Smokestacks frame the moon
as Nick and K race Burlington Street in the tank.
Nick tries not to talk about Carla.
K sees through him.

From the height of an overpass
they discover a factory blaze
and pull off at the next exit to watch.

They cruise up to the raging building like a drive-in
flames licking at the steady stars
and firefighters.

This is sharing.
Sitting in the flashing dark with hot coffee
and silence
between them.

FEAST

Nick learned to cook from his father
— that is, he learned to heat things —

he slides frozen pizza into a slow oven
watches congealed tins of meatballs and gravy
splutter molten in undersized pots

this fridge has never known a fresh vegetable
the freezer is stacked with hues of ground meat
a frosted trench of bargain perogies,
a stockade of microwave dinners

Nick plucks one from the front
and watches its slow inflation as it spins

the numbers pace their way down
his life here is always waiting

Punch clocks
Alarm clocks
Three-minute rounds

Suddenly, he remembers Kasia saying

Waiting is what will steal your life
and it's logically a state of dissatisfaction

He sniffs and goes upstairs for a sleep
leaving the soggy box untouched

*

unable to sink
to spread senses wide enough
for sleep
Nick has laid awake all night

called in sick
poured a piping soup thermos
with coffee
taken a joint from Chad
and gone to sit by the green
blue brown mirror
that puffs tiny
September mornings
against his face and forearms

Nick puffs gently too
burning the joint back slow
with hot mouthfuls of bitter coffee
watching delighted retirees
amble porcelain boats
white points of sails ducking
across the sun-sparked water
he flicks the nub
and takes down the dregs
and sits in unsurrounded presence

DOCKWORKER'S SONG

When I breathe
my smoker's lungs
mimic the sea

I've crossed the world
and it's all the same
strings of orange lights at night
silly differences by day
convenient steel mills in Hamilton
a plausible tower in Toronto
cold miles of water everywhere else

longshoremen stalk and bark
and squeeze popping fists
hook belt buckles with thumbs
and spit tar from black lungs

I've spent years clattering
like a squirrel on the roof
of the sea

I've spent a fortune on nothing
in places that are nowhere
with men who'll never remember
themselves
let alone each other

I've forgotten everything
that's ever happened to me

WEIGHT
Carla

The steelfires flood clouds
under the white-point torches of so few stars.

Everything here is expedience.
Nothing exists without some express use
in the great factory of things.

Nick has gone inside
to check on the pizza he's heating;
I'm draining a water-bottle and sweating it back out.

The air in this place has weight;
a breath through the gauze of summer.

The new worry of grief in me finds this place kindred,
but maybe I've spent my life blind to commonplace fears.

Nick's father — what we might become
when grief wounds us
leaves us dying for the rest of our lives.

CYCLE

Nick shoots over curbs and sewer grates
cold lacerations of rain
air taken in the snipped hisses of the gym
narrowed elbows through the alley
and then a boy's skid in the backyard
to ditch the bike by the fire escape

the whole time thinking of eating
then eating thinking of napping
then napping thinking of sparring
and then

work again

FUCKING
Carla

We push this bed across a mile of floor
cloud windows like a gym in February
map my navy blue sheets with salt
leopard print each other's shoulders
and stretch and bend and sprain
we shook the clanging stove until it nearly broke
through an anthology of positions
and even chipped Nick's tooth once on mine

spit the bits into my bed and laughed
you were never a pretty-boy anyway

WIDOW

The widow is where she always is,
the paned perch of her second floor sunroom,
backyard spread before her
a buffet of other lives.
Even the retired are children to her,
she has none of her own,
solitary and final in this world.
Her life is the flare of the lighter
to the cigarettes she burns down in halves,
the hot water that replaces her tea,
the stove's single working burner
warming her chicken noodle soup.

She will watch
arthritic joints petrify
and she becomes the laughter
and the cries
of the children she never had.

SWITCH

Nick watches the bouncer forcing someone out

one hand shackles a wrist
the other on his neck
the lock step cadence and then the shove

the drunk's righting himself
— no reeling — pause-angling
the dizzy world flat
he turns and springs

Nick's heart quickens
with the dull thump
of the bouncer's fist

the drunk falling
casual and ridiculous as death itself

the crack of a brain off the sidewalk
sound of a boiled egg hitting the floor

suppressed gasps

the boys are smoking
and looking at one another
cracking necks and knuckles
above the unnatural splay

and Nick hears the raccoons
continue to rummage

STAGNANT

Nick

The vindictive heat
and the irritable bead-sweating cabby
whose smoker's breath sounds like wind in a flag
who bitched about us into his cell
the whole way to and from the beer store
are the same.

Hate us; want us to suffer.

Even the beer hates us
warm buck a bottle shit
and conversation has pretty well told
our hangover headaches and hair of the dog
slurring to fuck off.

We've been drinking too long
and it's all horrible and sober again, like marriage.

K and I don't even want to be around ourselves
let alone each other. It's aggravation in a bottle,
directionless frustration, like three hours till work ends
when you can't take another minute.

And that's when the ugliness clears in my head —
and it makes sense all of a sudden
and I can bear it because I understand it.

K's not looking at me. Or, he's looking
but he isn't thinking of elsewhere.
He's right here with the shit bothering him.

The only reason we stay
is we've been here for years.

And the reason we're really hating it
is that there's nothing between either of us
but stagnant loyalty.

K asks where the fuck I'm off to
when I get up and walk off with two beers.
I know he doesn't give a shit, so I say nothing.
I just walk off so we can both feel better.

BOUNCER'S SONG

the danger comes from anywhere
and the thousand nights
I've stood bored and angry
I've meditated on my fear
and I can say
it has no content

like worry

like pain

I've seen pool cues snapped over knees and stabbed to a scarlet
    point
stalagmite bottle-ends ground into faces
chairs swung two-handed that scatter clattering shards of teeth
thumbs gouging, the eye making a sucking sound
women fighting, one hand in the other's hair, the other a reddening
    claw
prison-built arms and ink-webbed elbows put a popping squeeze
    around choking necks
skinny weasels smile around cigarettes then knife a disarmed
    moment in the gut
bone-bodied codgers, hair like old lady perms, go toe-to-toe like
    they were twenty-one with hard-ons

but watching that boy's head crack on the sidewalk
I knew it'd be jail for good for me,
that I'd have to go home

and open up my wrists in the tub

NEMESIS

Sunday night barroom
becomes an auditory hallucination
a slow black spin
when K shuts his eyes.

K's drunk himself invisible
falls forward
off the stool into a machine stumble
mumbles a drowned goodbye

fumbles outside in a flicker-stall
then goes still in the silence — distant ringing —
and dubiously falling into the car hood
a gross comedy of key drops,
groping and collisions
head against his own bumper

the door gives and he collapses in
folding awkwardly but numb
into the driverseat, finds the key he needs
then a sleepy deep breath in the quiet
before overpumping the gas
and the tank is alive in a hoarse roar.

Gearing stirs the world.

There are lost moments
the roll of streetlights overhead
he keeps trying to watch
sailing — graceful ease — out
at the freight train of parked cars
strung along the street.
Numb fear suddenly
as he breaks the careen in a sharp lunge

back to the middle of his lane.

He leans forward again
and the clip-bang of a mirror
smacked clean off then the road centre again
muttering, "Too much... Fuck"

another easing curve of drunken calculus
detonating impact — the arch smashed straight
violent clash of physics against smooth abstraction
spark bursting grind and metallic scream.

★

Morning finds a hangover like fish hooks in the throat
tremors and sweats, brain an open wound
swelling in the compress of his skull.

An empty dread has K shirtless
out at the curb, the car lurched
one wheel way up over it, crawling
beached across the sidewalk in agony.

Slit-eyed view of the jagged scarring
crooked concave of the car door,
paint scraped bare or to pockmarks.

Soon K will be gone back inside
to drunk-dream the nemesis
out there somewhere cruising angrily
in search of a mutilated twin.

IN ALLISTON

When the phone's hung up with a numb hand
the rye bottle almost unscrews itself
and an easing hour later
there's singing with the stereo
and spilling a careless little on the shirt
that doesn't matter at all
and the floor that matters less.

A thousand crickets
invoke a wall of sound
as he lurches from the weathered porch.
The whisky and noise
become fresh air and stars.

He wanders into fields,
throwing punches
then splays himself star-wise.

Looking at the sky,
knowing real dark,
he turns the last of the rye
to the soil.

These are the spells
of whisky, cricket song,
and a moon hung low like a sickle,
about to cleave the horizon.

A moon that has seen all lives pass.

TWO DAYS LATER

The sun has risen and fallen twice
and she's barely moved from bed.

Lumbering hollow-headed
to scoop meager handfuls that nauseate her
from a dwindling cereal box,

her strength is gone,
her muscles feel stringy
her taut skin and fierce eyes
pitted with surrender.

Her alarm clock drones
irrelevant talk radio
and the emptiness of loss.

When she finally answers the phone
her voice is a lost person's.

She does not even listen,
submerged beneath a surface.

My father, she says. Cancer.
Six months.

Nick is already racing for his bike.

DROP
Carla

Three days like Ophelia
and I return to myself a little.

Barely walking
sight is a tunnel
I find the registrar's building,

mind across a bracken country
on broken sky, the house
and land that require me.

I don't look at the lady behind the desk
but get the words out
and more numb tears while I'm at it.

My steps home are shallow
Kasia spoon-feeds me.

First I've eaten in a day

I'm relearning to swallow

as I suppose
I will have to relearn
everything.

NICK FINDS CARLA ASLEEP WITH JOURNAL OPEN ON HER CHEST
Carla

I have a life to assume.
Bigger than me, it requires me.
A life I would share with you, Macfarlane.

THIS MORNING

Trains bare against the sky
or hooded in hangars
or grinding slow, gather like will.

Heavy trucks press the highways;
entourages of spinning, cawing gulls
follow cargo ships that slide on the water like tracks,
and all the great cities are gathered
against their shores
waiting to receive them:

everything this morning is becoming.

Nick laces gutted steel toes,
mind moving as slow
as the inching ships in the harbour.

The place he has always been,
has slipped into a present
and expectant
elsewhere.

*

A calico sniffs around the corner of the house
jogs in snip steps to Carla's feet
its hungry purr tracing
the underside of her legs

She has no more tears

Nick sails the corner
duffel across his shoulder
ditches his bike and bag in one motion
and folds her to him
tiny all at once
warm breath through his shirt

Kasia pulls up
horn-rimmed chauffeur
in the back Nick and Carla curl together

no word from anyone
they have the journey to talk

K'S NORTH END

Sore everywhere
thumb punching
at the cordless
hunch on the porch

everything still
in the late afternoon
everything static

hungover all day
calling Nick again
even the dial tone hurts

no answer

even the sun isn't moving
even the car that pulls up

memory tries a feeble cinch
then there's disbelief

car nearly nudges the tank
the scarred twin facing it down

three guys coming out
brass knuckles and childhood horrors

leer twisting my gut
Hey, K! *You* still tough?

ACKNOWLEDGEMENTS

This book would not have been possible without Michael Holmes, who I rightly believed was the best editor for me before he had ever heard of me. It also could not have happened without a passing comment from Ken Harvey, who offhandedly suggested I turn a short story about boxing in the North End into a book. Both of you have been hugely helpful to me and in ways you may not realise. Thank you.

I'm also grateful to my family. To my parents and to Callie and Kevin.

The following people, in one way or another contributed to the writing of this book. Generally their support was moral but for someone like myself, that's by far the most important kind of support: Ali Hejripour, Lindsay Wilson, Jenn Doherty, Peter Fraser, Andrea McKenzie, Shosh Levitt, Angela Rawlings, James Ho, Marina Mandal, Eddie Gebbie, Shannon Russell, Jenny Banks, Claire Leewing, Irene Lum, Didi Ohri, Shanaeh Reid, Phillip Ennis, and everyone at C.W. Jefferys.

I wish to gratefully acknowledge the financial support of the Toronto Arts Council and the Ontario Arts Council's Writers' Reserve. I'm also very grateful to the Leighton Studios at the Banff Arts Centre for allowing me a very productive stay during the writing of this book.